P9-AOK-769

JAN 14 1999

B J   92,860
Malone
Rekela, George
Karl Malone: star forward

                              19.95

Kinsman Free Public Library
Kinsman, Ohio

DISCARDED

1. Books may be kept two weeks and may be renewed
once for the same.
2. A fine is charged for each day a book is not returned
according to the above rule.
3. All injuries to books beyond reasonable wear and all
losses shall be made good to the satisfaction of the
Librarian.
4. Each borrower is held responsible for all books drawn
on his card and for all fines accruing on the same.

DEMCO

Karl Malone

Karl Malone

Star Forward

George Rekela

Enslow Publishers, Inc.

44 Fadem Road	PO Box 38
Box 699	Aldershot
Springfield, NJ 07081	Hants GU12 6BP
USA	UK

KINSMAN FREE PUBLIC LIBRARY
6420 CHURCH STREET
P.O. BOX 166
KINSMAN, OHIO 44428

DISCARDED

92,860

Copyright © 1998 by George Rekela.

All rights reserved.

No part of this book may be reproduced by any means
without the written permission of the publisher.

Library of Congress Cataloging-in-Publication Data

Rekela, George R., 1943–
        Karl Malone: star forward / George Rekela.
            p.   cm. — (Sports reports)
        Includes bibliographical references (p.) and index.
    Summary: Profiles the personal life and professional career of the
    Utah Jazz player who is one of the NBA's premier forwards.
        ISBN 0-89490-931-2
        1. Malone, Karl—Juvenile literature. 2. Basketball players—
    United States—Biography—Juvenile literature. 3. Utah Jazz
    (Basketball team)—Juvenile literature. [1. Malone, Karl.
    2. Basketball players. 3. Utah Jazz (Basketball team) 4. Afro-Americans—
    Biography.] I. Series.
    GV884.M18R45   1998
    796.323′092—dc21
    [B]   97-25560
                                                                      CIP
                                                                       AC

Printed in the United States of America.

10 9 8 7 6 5 4 3 2 1

Photo Credits: © Brian Drake, pp. 10, 45, 53, 58, 80; George Rekela, pp. 12,
17, 42, 51, 64, 70, 74, 86, 93; Louisiana Tech Sports Information Photo, pp. 21,
28, 32; NCAA Archives, p. 34.

Cover Photo: © Brian Drake

Contents

Chapter 1

An All-Star Appearance

The Delta Center is the crown jewel in the Salt Lake City skyline. It is in this beautiful 19,911-seat arena that the sports fans of Utah come to experience the wonder, the skill, and the magic of the state's only major-league sports team, the National Basketball Association's (NBA's) Utah Jazz.

Construction of the Delta Center began on June 11, 1990, and was completed sixteen months later in October 1991. Located within walking distance of downtown stores, restaurants, and Salt Lake City's famed Temple Square, the Delta Center is a $66 million tribute to the people of Utah, their love of professional basketball, and the Jazz.

Although the Jazz did not have a regular-season

home game scheduled for February 21, 1993, the Delta Center was packed to the rafters anyway. Most of the Jazz players had the night off. The team's two star players, Karl Malone and John Stockton, would be busy, however. They had been selected to play in the annual NBA All-Star Game that night, and the eyes and ears of sports fans everywhere would be focused on this game.

Shortly after the Delta Center opened, NBA Commissioner David Stern announced it would be home to the 1993 All-Star Game. The city earned the honor as a result of its unwavering support of the Jazz since the franchise moved to Salt Lake City from New Orleans in 1979.

The Jazz struggled in their first six seasons in Utah, but then something totally unforeseen happened. In the first round of the NBA college draft, the Jazz selected little-known forward Karl Malone from Louisiana Tech University. Little was expected of Malone when he traveled to Salt Lake City. He would soon prove all the experts wrong. Utah's consecutive string of successes in the NBA's Midwest Division started with Malone's arrival, and it continues to this day. Malone has proven himself to be one of the best power forwards in the game today.

Starting at power forward in the annual NBA All-Star Game had become routine for Malone by

1993. This All-Star Game would be different. It would be played in the Delta Center. For Malone and teammate John Stockton, this would be a home game.

Sweat glistened on Malone's body as he took a pass from Stockton and headed toward the basket. A defender blocked his path, but only briefly, as Malone reached out with his free hand and swept him aside. Now the big power forward was airborne, sailing unimpeded toward the basket. Malone slammed the ball through the hoop, and the full house at the Delta Center exploded in a chorus of cheering.

"If you ever want to do well," Malone told reporters before the game, "you definitely want to do well at home."[1] Home for Malone was the Delta Center, and he was playing before his people. "My whole thing is," he said, "I'm afraid to let people down."[2] Karl Malone would not let any Utah resident down this evening. He was one of the best players on the floor.

Karl Malone scored 12 first-quarter points. This is difficult to accomplish in a game where players constantly shuttle in and out of the contest. Chaos at an All-Star Game can result when coaches attempt to give every player equal time on the floor. Play can get ragged, especially considering the fact that both teams practice for just forty-five minutes the day

FACT

Karl Malone has averaged 11 rebounds per game throughout his professional career.

1985–86	8.9 rebounds
1986–87	10.4 rebounds
1987–88	12.0 rebounds
1988–89	10.7 rebounds
1989–90	11.1 rebounds
1990–91	11.8 rebounds
1991–92	11.2 rebounds
1992–93	11.2 rebounds
1993–94	11.5 rebounds
1994–95	10.6 rebounds
1995–96	9.8 rebounds
1996–97	9.9 rebounds

Hometown fans cheered Karl Malone as he played in the 1993 NBA All-Star Game at the Delta Center in Salt Lake City.

before. The best players will rise to the occasion. Utah fans were counting on Malone, and he did not disappoint them.

Karl Malone's 28 points and 10 rebounds, combined with John Stockton's 15 assists, allowed the West to win the game. The fans went home with memories of great performances.

What made the game truly memorable was the way it ended. Michael Jordan, Mark Price, and Patrick Ewing of the East team nearly ruined the Malone-Stockton show. Price made 3 three-pointers in the final three minutes of the third quarter, and then, with the West leading, 101–95, with less than seven minutes remaining in the contest, he made two more to tie the score, 103–103.

Led by Malone and Stockton, the West team built the lead back to five with less than a minute remaining in the game. Few fans headed for the exits, for they realized the explosive power of the East's scoring machine. The red-hot Price sank a three-pointer that closed the gap to 117–115, with twenty-six seconds left. Then Jordan was fouled and sank one of two free-throw attempts. Golden State's Tim Hardaway of the West took the ball across the midcourt line and was fouled. Like Jordan, he was able to convert only one of his two free throw shots. The score was 118–116, with the West in the lead.

Intense play at both ends of the court has made Karl Malone—shown here locking up with Minnesota's Kevin Garnett—one of the most-respected players in the NBA.

The East called a timeout with eight seconds showing on the clock. Price then lobbed the ball in to Ewing, who scored the tying basket on a baseline jumper. This put the game into overtime.

Malone set the pace from the start of the overtime period. He took a pass from Stockton and, without hesitation, drove through the lane, past Ewing, for an easy layup. The West's Dan Majerle then hit a three-pointer with three minutes left in overtime. This put his team ahead to stay. Then Stockton added a layup and scored on an outside jumper. Charles Barkley made a three-pointer, and the West led, 131–125, with 1:32 left. When the East pulled to within three points, Stockton provided a key steal with only fifteen seconds showing on the clock. The final score was 135–132, West. Malone and Stockton were mobbed by fans at the final buzzer. It was the greatest moment in the Salt Lake City community's sports history. As a worldwide audience watched the game on television, two Utah Jazz players led the NBA West All-Star team to victory.

As their reward, Malone and Stockton were named co-Most Valuable Players. This was only the second time that two players had shared this honor in an NBA All-Star Game. (Elgin Baylor and Bob Pettit were the first, sharing the honor after the 1959 game.)

Chapter 2

The Malone Era

Salt Lake City, Utah, was the farthest place from young Karl Malone's mind when he was growing up in Summerfield, Louisiana, a tiny hamlet located a few miles south of the Arkansas-Louisiana state line.

Born in Summerfield on July 24, 1963, to J. P. and Shirley Malone, Karl was the second youngest of nine children. Karl's mother became a single parent after Karl's father died, when Karl was just three years old.

To support her large family, Shirley Malone immediately went to work for two employers—a local sawmill and a nearby poultry plant. She simply figured it was her duty as a mother to provide for her children. "It was my responsibility," she

FACT

Karl Malone provides financial support for homeless shelters and child-abuse prevention centers in the Salt Lake City metropolitan area. He also buys fifty tickets to each Jazz home game and gives them to underprivileged young people.

would say in later years. "I believe every tub should sit on its own bottom."[1] During daytime hours, Shirley would run a forklift at the sawmill. After her shift was over, she would go to the poultry plant and cut up chickens. Somehow she found time to cook and clean for her family and for a neighbor's family.

"I saw my mother put cardboard in her shoes to cover up the holes," Karl Malone said, "just so each of us could have a good pair."[2] Water and mud would soak through the cardboard in Shirley Malone's shoes, but she never complained. On weekends, she would take the family fishing and hunting. Highway signs in Louisiana refer to the state as a "sportsman's paradise." Karl's mother did not fish for sport; she and her kids fished for food for their table. She also was an expert with a rifle and, in autumn months, brought home game birds she had shot, dressed, and prepared for eating.

Using her wages from the sawmill and poultry facility and the fish and game birds she bagged, Shirley Malone kept her family going. Karl never considered himself to be poor. His family was rich in ways others could never have imagined.

The family had purchased an old basketball long before Karl was born. He started playing with it soon after he learned to walk. Shirley Malone would

Though his NBA days were still far away, as a young boy Karl Malone could often be found with a basketball in his hands.

hold out her arms like a hoop while young Karl shot baskets through them. Karl's maternal grandfather stood six feet nine inches tall, so it was no surprise when Karl began growing like a weed. Soon Karl's mother had to stand on a chair with her arms in a circle to create a basket. The ball would bounce off her chest, and she reacted by throwing back her head in laughter.

"A lot of people would pass by," Malone remembered, "and say, 'What is she doing?'" They told Shirley Malone she was foolish, that her youngest son would never amount to anything. "Well, I guess they were wrong," said Malone.[3] "We did everything the old-fashioned way," he remembered.[4] But soon he was too big for shooting at a basket created by his mother's arms.

"We got an old bicycle tire, knocked the spokes out of it, and put hay wire on it. That was our new basket." Karl and his brothers then cut down an old oak tree and used it to make a backboard. "We'd play on dirt—red clay that got all over our shoes, our clothes, and everything."[5]

Karl's mother married the local plumber, Ed Turner, in 1975. The couple subsequently went into business for themselves when they opened Turner's Groceteria and Washateria in Summerfield. The unusual name was selected because the business was a combination general store, self-service laundry, and restaurant. Life got easier for Karl's mother after that, and she quit her jobs at the sawmill and poultry plant.

Meanwhile, Karl and his brother Terry were growing up. Once, when they thought no one was watching, the two brothers stole some watermelons from a neighbor's patch. To further aggravate the situation, the boys smashed some melons they had not stolen. The neighbor had witnessed it all and promptly reported the theft and vandalism to the boys' mother. She responded by making Karl and Terry chop wood for the man every day for six weeks. The brothers were also required to prepare his fireplace and light the fire every night.[6]

As a young boy, Karl was taller and stronger than other boys his age. He saw them outdoors playing football during fall afternoons and asked his mother if he could join them. She would have none of it. Football, Shirley Malone Turner believed, was a brutal and dehumanizing sport. "I could see that her mind was made up. I never thought about football again," said Karl Malone.[7]

Karl would have to get his exercise elsewhere. His mother got him a job wrestling two-hundred-pound hogs on a ranch. Karl was assigned the task of subduing the animals so that rings could be put in their noses. When he did, the hogs were chained up easily. Young Karl's arms soon grew to the size of tree trunks.

All of the Malone boys exceeded average height and played basketball whenever they could. The games grew in intensity. "If I didn't play," said Karl Malone, "I was looked upon as some kind of freak."[8] Dan Malone, eight years older than Karl, dominated the family games and bullied the youngster into playing. "My brother used to be rough with me on purpose," Malone said. "I would shoot the ball, and he would hit me for no reason." But Dan Malone did have a reason. He wanted to toughen up their mother's "mama's boy."[9]

"I would cry," said Malone, "but he would call me a little sissy. Then I would get fighting mad."[10] Karl had a temper in those days, and it would often come out in those backyard games. But eventually he learned how to transfer his anger into intensity going up against big brother Dan. Soon he was outplaying him and could think of little else than facing him in basketball combat the next day.

Karl Malone quickly became hooked on basketball, but not on schoolbooks. His grades in junior high school and high school were average, not up to his mother's high standards. "I let my mother down," Malone said of his life between ninth and

Karl Malone's talents as a basketball player became evident while he was in high school, drawing the attention of several coaches.

twelfth grades.[11] He was now playing organized basketball at Summerfield High, and the game had become his obsession. His personality had also changed. He and his friends and teammates were known in Summerfield as the "neighborhood busters." They frequently got themselves in trouble with their mischief.

Only on the basketball court could Karl properly channel his energy. He changed from a back-alley hacker into a shooter with a light touch. He developed smooth skills on the basketball court that set him apart from his teammates and opponents. Led by Malone in 1980–81, Summerfield High School won its division in the Louisiana state tournament. College scouts began to take an interest in Malone. The next year, representatives of major college basketball power-houses such as Louisiana State University, Memphis State, and Arkansas were calling.

Summerfield dominated Louisiana high school basketball circles during the so-called Malone Era in the state. With Karl averaging 30 points and 20 rebounds per game, his team waltzed to its third consecutive championship. The big-time college recruiters who had flocked to Summerfield's games were gone, however. The problem was Karl's grades. He had slipped below a C average. His grade point average was not good enough for him to play college basketball as a freshman.

Yet, in his own words, he "got pretty cocky" in his senior high school season. He knew he had superior talent on the basketball court and figured that was enough. He started cutting classes and abandoned his studies.

"I knew I was good, and no one could tell me otherwise. I was the big hero in my high school."[12] Hero worship cost Karl. His reputation changed from that of a cute mama's boy to that of an insufferable brat. "I was beginning to think that I was special and better than other people."[13] As a result, schoolwork finished a poor second in his life. It cost him the 1981–82 college basketball season.

Chapter 3

Life at Louisiana Tech

Louisiana Tech University is in Ruston, a city nestled in the piney woods and hills in the northern part of the state. Before the turn of the twentieth century, the Ruston area was known mainly for the production of peaches and poultry. Louisiana Tech University soon saw to it that the hills became fruitful in other ways as well. A strong tradition of academic excellence was cultivated on the 950 acres that encompassed Louisiana Tech. The college quickly grew in enrollment from 196 in its first year of operation to more than ten thousand students by the time eighteen-year-old Karl Malone first set foot on campus.

Malone arrived at college in the fall of 1981. He had to wait a year before he would be able to play for the Louisiana Tech Bulldogs, however. His low grades in his senior year of high school kept him from that first year of competition while he spent time in college classrooms trying to achieve the required C average. "Not only did I let my family down," he said, "I let myself down." When he enrolled at Louisiana Tech, his life clearly was at a crossroads. "I didn't want to be a loser."[1]

He recalled that sometime after his high school graduation, he looked directly into a mirror and asked himself out loud: "Karl, are you going to be a loser for the rest of your life, or are you going to do something positive with yourself?" His reflection answered back: "Karl Malone will never be a loser again."[2]

He selected a small school close to home and chose elementary education as his college major. Working with children had always interested him, and majoring in education was also a way for him to recapture some of the time he himself had wasted in the classroom. He wanted to be a teacher, and he sensed that he could be a good teacher. Before long, he had earned a grade point average of 2.6 at Louisiana Tech.

During his freshman year, on those rare moments when he had some free time, he would slip off by himself and shoot baskets at a vacant campus gym. Often the only sound heard in the building was the bouncing of Malone's basketball on the gym floor.

Coach Andy Russo knew of Karl Malone's struggles in the classroom and his anguish at having to sit out a year. Russo had come to Louisiana Tech as head basketball coach in 1979 and saw the Bulldogs finish with a 17–10 record. The following season was, in Russo's words, "frustrating," not because of the team's lack of success (the Bulldogs won 20 games), but because the team had not drawn a National Collegiate Athletic Association (NCAA) or even a National Invitational Tournament (NIT) bid. Louisiana Tech, it seemed, was too far off the beaten track. The school had a reputation for women's basketball, but not men's. Russo hoped things would change. He knew that in Karl Malone, he had a player who could bring the Louisiana Tech men's program a national reputation. Unfortunately, while Malone sat out a season, the Bulldogs won only 11 games and lost 16.

By the time Louisiana Tech's 1982–83 season rolled around, Karl Malone had grown to fill out his six-foot nine-inch frame and weighed 250 pounds. His year away from active competition had not harmed his physical condition. In fact, he was more muscular and developed than he had been in high

FACT

Karl Malone is built more like a football tight end than a basketball forward. His size and strength make him difficult to defend in the low post. He also fills the lane on fast breaks and scores frequently on midrange jump shots.

Louisiana Tech basketball coach Andy Russo saw a lot of talent in Karl Malone. He was frustrated, though, that Malone had to sit out his freshman season due to poor grades.

school. He ached for the chance to prove his ability on the basketball court. Russo made him a starter instantly, and the Bulldogs won six of their first eight games, including exhibitions. Louisiana Tech won 19 of 28 games in Malone's first year, but still failed to gain national recognition. Malone was a one-man show, averaging 20.9 points per game, hitting on 217 out of 373 field goal attempts. He averaged 10.3 rebounds and 10 baskets per game.

Everything came together for Louisiana Tech, Coach Russo, and Karl Malone in the 1983–84 season. "It was like a five-month history lesson," Russo recalled, "as we hurdled one milestone after another."[3] This was to be a record-setting campaign for the Bulldogs. It would eventually take the team further than Louisiana Tech had ever gone before.

The Bulldogs started off with an overtime win on the road against a formidable Western Kentucky team. The Bulldogs then defeated Rice University on the road a few nights later, and ran off seven consecutive wins to open the season. It was the team's longest winning streak since the 1971–72 season.

Louisiana Tech stumbled with two straight losses on the road (to Tennessee and Texas-El Paso). Then they ran off ten wins in their next eleven games to stand at 17 wins, 3 losses the first week of February 1984. Malone was on fire during this period. He scored 40 points at Centenary, 26 against Northwestern State, and 26 at home against McNeese State. NBA scouts began to sit up and take notice of this obscure northern Louisiana team and its star, Karl Malone.

Just when it seemed things could not get any better, the Bulldogs hit a speed bump. Tech lost three of four road conference games during a nine-day period. Russo, however, refused to panic. He told the team he would make no changes. He wanted them to continue playing the way they had earlier. Eventually the ball had to bounce their way.

Louisiana Tech finished the regular season with four straight victories and entered the conference tournament feeling rejuvenated and confident. They mowed down North Texas State, 92–68, in a first-round elimination game in Ruston, earning the right to advance to the semifinal round in Beaumont, Texas. Getting a season-high 18-point performance from unheralded Robert Godbolt, the Bulldogs raced past Northeast Louisiana, 69–56. The team then faced the unenviable task of going against host Lamar University for the conference title and the right to advance to the NCAA tournament.

Defeating Lamar would not be an easy task. The Cardinals were riding an eighty-game home winning streak that dated back six seasons (the longest string in college basketball history). Making things look even bleaker was the fact that Lamar had routed the Bulldogs, 85–60, in Beaumont just three weeks earlier.

The game was to be televised on the USA cable television network, the first time Louisiana Tech men's basketball would receive national coverage. Before this game, many pro scouts had heard the name Karl Malone, but they had never seen him play.

Louisiana Tech proved to be the hottest team that night as it raced past the stunned Lamar Cardinals. The Techmen were in control all night and won, 68–65, for the right to represent the Southland Conference in the NCAA tournament. Said Russo:

> We had been so close to the NCAA tournament three other times, particularly in 1981. Then, suddenly, there it was. Our team played a tremendous game to beat Lamar at their place. We just came out, got some confidence early and played like champions.[4]

The day after the Lamar victory, Malone and his teammates huddled around a television set to find out who and where the Bulldogs would be playing in the NCAA tournament. The answer came by midafternoon and pointed the team toward Memphis in the Midwest bracket. The Bulldogs

Improving with each passing year, Karl Malone led the Louisiana Tech Bulldogs team to its best performance ever in the NCAA tournament.

would be included in a six-team mix that pitted Tech against West Coast representative Fresno State.

The NCAA tournament would be Malone's chance to shine. He was averaging 18 points and 8 rebounds per game, and his team was going to be on national television. It seemed to him as if everything he had done in his life so far had led him to this game. He vowed to meet the challenge.

Earlier in the year, a Louisiana sportswriter had labeled Malone "the Mailman." When asked why, the writer responded, "Because Malone delivers."[5] Few nicknames in sports have stuck so rapidly. On the campus of Louisiana Tech and throughout the state, Malone was "the Mailman." It was time for him to deliver in Memphis.

Malone singlehandedly destroyed Fresno State. He propelled the Bulldogs to a first-half lead at the Mid-South Coliseum. In the second half, it was all Malone as he jammed in basket after basket and completely controlled both backboards. He finished with 24 points and 12 rebounds in a 66–56 Louisiana Tech victory. Many pro scouts watching that day penciled in the name Karl Malone as a potential first-round NBA draft choice.

The dream of an NCAA championship for Malone and the Bulldogs died in the next round. Akeem Olajuwon (as he spelled his first name at that time), and the powerful Houston Cougars stopped the Bulldogs, 77–69. Karl Malone and Rennie Bailey shared scoring honors, with 18 points each. "We really didn't play too badly against Houston," remembered Russo. "I don't believe they intimidated us, but it was a new and tense situation that our guys had not experienced."[6]

When the Olympic trials began that summer, Karl Malone was introduced to another promising athlete from a small college. His name was John Stockton, and he had just finished up his college career at tiny Gonzaga University in Spokane, Washington. Six-foot one-inch Stockton was the first

Though he did not make the 1984 Olympic Team, Karl Malone (back row, second from left) represented his country along with future Dream Team member Charles Barkley (front row, far right) at the 1983 World University Games, helping his team bring home the bronze medal.

player in Gonzaga history to score 1,000 points with 500 or more assists. Later he would be drafted in the first round by the NBA's Utah Jazz. Bobby Knight, head coach at Indiana University, served as coach of the United States Olympic team that year. He was determined to win the gold medal for America. Karl Malone and John Stockton went all out and did their best to help him. Both of them desperately wanted to be in the Olympics, but it was not to be. Neither of them made the team. This would not be their only basketball disappointment together. Malone's and Stockton's Olympic dreams did not die, however.

Back at Louisiana Tech, Coach Russo was full of optimism for the upcoming season. "No matter how talented or determined you are," he said, "the experience of being in the NCAA tournament helps tremendously."[7] He looked forward to a return trip in 1985.

The Bulldogs took the league championship and had a chance to win the NCAA tournament. Malone averaged 16.5 points and 9 rebounds per game in his final season in college. He saved his best for his last three games at Louisiana Tech. The Bulldogs' first-round opponent in the 1985 NCAA tournament was the University of Pittsburgh. With Malone and teammate Willie Simmons controlling the backboards, the Bulldogs ran to a 37–20 halftime lead and never looked back. Louisiana Tech won, 78–54. Malone and Simmons had 10 rebounds each. This was nearly the total amount compiled by the entire Pittsburgh team.

In the other bracket, the Ohio State University Buckeyes roared past Iowa State, 75–64, to set up a meeting with the Bulldogs. Facing a Big Ten team in the NCAA tournament solidified the Louisiana Tech men's basketball team's legitimacy. The final score was Louisiana Tech 79, Ohio State 67, but the game was not as close as the score seemed to indicate. Malone and Louisiana Tech overwhelmed the Buckeyes. Malone crashed the boards for 14 rebounds and 22 points. Every NBA scout knew about Karl Malone now, and most wanted him for their first draft pick. All doubts about his not being able to perform against high-quality opposition vanished after his showing against Ohio State.

The win over the Buckeyes advanced Louisiana Tech to the Sweet Sixteen of the NCAA tournament. Only sixteen teams remained, and four victories would bring the championship to the Bulldogs. "It's Tech's turn to deliver the knockout punch," Coach Russo said.[8]

The knockout punch came, but it was Tech on the receiving end. In the most heartbreaking of finishes, Oklahoma, a Big Eight team, defeated the

FACT

In 1996 Karl Malone surpassed Alex English's record of eight seasons in a row with 2,000 or more points.

Bulldogs, 86–84 in overtime in the NCAA Midwest Regional semifinal game. Oklahoma, coached by Billy Tubbs and led by All-American Wayman Tisdale, led at the half, 32–28. Louisiana Tech, led by Malone's successful twenty-five-foot jump shots, stormed back to take the lead, only to see regulation time end in a 74–74 tie. Malone finished with 20 points and an astonishing 16 rebounds. It was not enough to win the game, though.

Malone averaged 19.6 points and 12 rebounds in five NCAA tournament games in 1984 and 1985. For Karl Malone, it was now time to give professional basketball a try.

Chapter 4

Drafted by the Jazz

The Utah Jazz was an NBA team born out of frustration. Salt Lake City had lost its professional basketball team, the Utah Stars, when the Stars and the old American Basketball Association (ABA) ceased operations in 1976. There seemed to be no good reason for Salt Lake City to have another pro basketball team—until the NBA New Orleans Jazz started to have attendance problems. An NBA expansion team since 1974, the New Orleans Jazz were headed by a nine-man group chaired by Fred Rosenfeld. He paid $6.2 million so the Jazz could become the eighteenth member of the NBA.

On April 10, 1979, Jazz management announced plans to move the Jazz from New Orleans to Salt

Lake City. The transfer was approved by the NBA Board of Governors on June 8, 1979. The team would keep the name Jazz.

The team arrived in Utah with nondescript players such as Ben Poquette, Allan Bristow, and Duck Williams, and the first edition of the Utah Jazz lost 58 games in 1979–80. Even worse was the fact that the team averaged only 7,821 in attendance at Salt Lake City's historic Salt Palace. The previous year, the New Orleans Jazz's attendance average was 8,883. No matter where it played, this seemed to be a franchise in trouble.

The Jazz selected Darrell Griffith from the University of Louisville as their first-round draft pick. Griffith had been College Player of the Year, but he could not turn the team around. The Jazz won 28 games and lost 54 in 1980–81. The team stumbled through two more losing seasons until 1983–84, when they made the playoffs for the first time in team history. Attendance problems continued to plague the franchise, however. The Jazz once again averaged fewer than ten thousand spectators per game. The team even received permission to play some "home" games in Las Vegas, Nevada, in hopes of boosting attendance.

Then something happened in Salt Lake City that eventually would be instrumental in turning the franchise around. The Jazz selected John Stockton of Gonzaga University in Spokane, Washington, in the 1984 NBA college draft. Stockton had averaged 12.5 points per game at Gonzaga, but he was not drafted to be a scorer. He would be an assist man, the one who sets up the scorer. The only problem: the Jazz did not have a scorer. He would arrive one year later in the person of Karl Malone from Louisiana Tech University.

When Karl Malone entered the NBA draft, he expected to be one of the first five college players picked. Utah was drafting in the thirteenth position, so Malone never suspected he would be selected by the Jazz. Malone saw players such as Keith Lee, Joe Kleine, Jon Koncak, and Kenny Green chosen ahead of him. He began to wonder if anyone would select him.

"I wanted to do some stuff for my mom, and I wanted to get out on my own," he said. "I grew up quite a bit in college, but I wasn't where I wanted to be. It was time for me to grow up all the way. It was time to get away from home."[1]

He did not sleep at all the night before the June 18, 1985, draft. "I thought for sure Dallas was going to take me. In fact, I remember telling my mom, 'I'm moving to Dallas.'"[2]

The New York Knicks drafted first and selected

FACT

At one time, Karl Malone owned and operated an eighteen-wheel tandem trailer-truck.

Patrick Ewing. Next Waymon Tisdale went to the Indiana Pacers. The third player selected was Benoit Benjamin, who went to the Clippers. Next was Xavier McDaniel, who went to Seattle.

Dallas was to pick eighth. "I was already moving off my seat," Malone said. "Then I heard the announcer say that Dallas had drafted Detlef Schrempf. Wow."[3] Reality struck Malone like a bolt of lightning. It got worse. Four other teams

The fortunes of the troubled Utah Jazz franchise began to improve when they selected Gonzaga University's John Stockton in the 1984 NBA college draft. Stockton would go on to become one of the best assist-makers in NBA history.

announced their selections. Karl Malone was not mentioned. "Then I started thinking, 'Hey what if nobody drafts me?' I started getting a little frightened."[4] The fear ended on the thirteenth pick, when Utah selected him.

Utah offered Malone a contract that would pay him $250,000 per year. Malone felt insulted. He threatened to leave the country and play professional basketball in Italy. Eventually Malone's agent and Utah management agreed on a contract that would pay him more. When he reported for training camp, however, he had a lot of work to do. Former Jazz coach Frank Layden recalled, "Malone had no intensity. I said, 'Now I know why we got him as the 13th pick.' He just didn't play hard."[5]

Other NBA experts thought that maybe the thirteenth spot was too high. They pointed to the fact that Malone's scoring average had declined each year he was in college. What they did not take into consideration was the fact that each year Malone played in college, the Louisiana Tech Bulldogs had improved as a team and did not have to rely on him as much for scoring. "We needed a power forward badly," Layden said, "and this kid filled the bill perfectly."[6] But would Malone make it?

His mother knew what was wrong. "He was homesick," she told writer Cameron Stauth.

Malone's days in the Jazz training camp were miserable. Utah was full of snowcapped mountains and strange people. "That first month he was there, we had a $700 telephone bill. He wanted to come home. I told him, 'Sugar, that's your job now.'" His mother would not allow him to quit basketball and come home.[7]

The Jazz lost their first two regular-season games, and Malone played poorly. Then, on November 30, 1985, in Oakland, California, something happened. Karl Malone scored 18 points, to lead the Jazz past the Golden State Warriors, 89–88. He had studied the game for two months, picked up on its subtleties, and all of a sudden began throwing his weight around. He had become an imposing figure on the court.

"There are players who come into this league and they are who they are," commented Layden. "And you know that's what they're going to be. Karl is going to get better and better."[8] But not even Layden could guess how good Karl Malone would be.

Malone scored 25 points in a losing effort against the Seattle Supersonics, 91–84. Layden said, "I didn't know he'd become such a force in the league so quickly."[9] Malone was named Rookie of the Month for December.

Making an immediate impact in the NBA, Karl Malone helped the Utah Jazz reach the playoffs in his rookie season.

He was adjusting well to life in the NBA. His shooting and rebounding improved, but there was one area of deficiency—free-throw shooting. As a rookie, Karl Malone made only 48 percent of his free throws. Eventually, through hard work and determination, he would increase that figure to 72 percent.

The Jazz finished the season with 42 wins and 40 losses. The team advanced to the playoffs for the third straight year and faced the Dallas Mavericks, the team Malone had originally wanted to play for.

The NBA playoffs often bring out the best in players, and, in Karl Malone's case, the games inspired superior performance. He scored 23 points and pulled down 13 rebounds in a 101–98 loss in the first game at Dallas. His best game was the following night when he singed the nets for 31 points. However, the Jazz lost the series to the Mavericks, 3 games to one.

Chapter 5

The Ultimate Power Forward

With Karl Malone in town, the Utah Jazz never again missed the NBA playoffs. Malone matured as a player during the 1986–87 season in Salt Lake City. He led the team in scoring with an average of 21.7 points per game. He also averaged over 10 rebounds per game. The Salt Palace was now sold out for thirty-two Utah games. The Jazz won 44 and lost 38 for the second-best regular-season record in team history.

"Malone became the quintessential power forward—strong, fast, and nasty," wrote Cameron Stauth.[1] Karl Malone worked on reducing his body fat. Eventually he got it down to less than 5 percent. In addition, the league was showing him respect, something that had been missing in his rookie season.

The Jazz faced the Golden State Warriors in the 1987 playoffs. The Warriors seemed to be in awe of Malone for the first two games. They played like sleepwalkers, losing the first two games to the Jazz at the Salt Palace. In the end, it was Utah's turn to slump. This would be the start of a reputation that would haunt them for years. The Jazz lost the next three games to the Warriors, including a 118–113 loss at home, despite Malone's 23 points.

The series was not without controversy. Malone was grabbed by the Warriors' Greg Ballard for an intentional foul. When Malone casually flipped the ball in Ballard's direction as he walked to the free-throw line, Ballard took offense at this and hurled the ball back. A bench-clearing brawl started. Some fans even got involved. But Malone stood his ground.

After the deciding playoff game, reporter Kurt Kragthorpe asked Malone if he planned on becoming a better player. "I can improve," he replied, "but I'm not going to talk about improving. I'm just going to do it."[2]

True to his word, Karl Malone did improve on his performance. During the following season, 1987–88, he increased his scoring average by six points per game (to 27.7) and averaged 12 rebounds per game. The rest of the NBA took considerable notice. Meanwhile, the Jazz cranked it up a notch when fourth-year point guard John Stockton was moved into a starting role. Stockton led the NBA in assists, with 13.8 per game. Many of them went to Malone as he and Stockton developed into one of the top one-two punches in the history of basketball.

Stockton and Malone were both named to the All-NBA second team, and Karl Malone made the first in a long string of All-Star Game appearances. Malone led the West team in scoring (22 points) and rebounds (10 boards). Next, Stockton and Malone were selected as league players of the month for February and March, respectively.

Utah finished with 47 wins and 35 losses, closing the regular season with five consecutive victories. The team also set a record for most wins at home, with 33. The Jazz advanced to the playoffs to face Portland. After losing the first game, the Jazz swept the next three games to advance to the semifinals against the defending world champion Los Angeles Lakers.

Malone scored 29 points in the opener at the Forum in Los Angeles, but the Lakers coasted to a 111–91 win. Few gave the Jazz a chance against the Lakers. Led by another 29 points from Malone,

PROPERTY OF
KINSMAN FREE PUBLIC LIBRARY

however, Utah charged back for a 101–97 road win. The Jazz took a 2–1 series lead three nights later in Salt Lake City, with a 96–89 win. Again Malone scored 29.

Los Angeles, behind James Worthy, evened the series at 2–2 with a 113–100 win. For the fourth consecutive game, Malone recorded 29 points. This time he also led the Jazz in rebounding, with 11. The series returned to Los Angeles, and the Lakers, as expected, won to take a 3–2 lead. The Jazz did not go down meekly, however. At the Salt Palace, Malone scored 27 points and had 11 rebounds to pace Utah to a 108–80 drubbing of the mighty Lakers. The seventh and deciding game went to Los Angeles, 109–98. Malone totaled 31 points and 15 rebounds in the losing effort.

Confidence was high in Salt Lake City for the 1988–89 season. Coach Layden was made team president, and his assistant, Jerry Sloan, became the head coach. The Jazz went on to set a club record with 51 victories, but fell to Golden State in only three games in the first round of the playoffs.

The playoff setback was a bitter pill to swallow, especially with such high expectations in Salt Lake City. Fans could only reflect on Malone's season-high 44 points against Philadelphia on December 17. He added at least 40 points on three other occasions. In the three-game playoff disaster against the Warriors, Malone was the only shining star. He averaged 30.7 points and 16.3 rebounds.

The following season saw Malone voted to the NBA All-Star Team for the third straight year. He was unable to play, however, because of an ankle injury. Prior to the game, he had been named NBA Player of the Month for January. Malone finished second to Michael Jordan in scoring, with a 31-point average. "I think that when you first come into the league," Malone remarked, "you want to make a name for yourself. You want to prove to everybody that you can score and rebound."[3] Malone's personal high was

Jerry Sloan (center) became Karl Malone's coach in 1988, when he took over the head coaching duties for the Utah Jazz.

a 52-point game in a victory over the Charlotte Hornets on December 22, 1989. Then, on January 27, 1990, he set tongues wagging throughout the NBA with an incredible 61-point outburst in a game against the Milwaukee Bucks. In Utah's last twenty-six games of the regular season, Karl Malone led the club in scoring twenty-four times.

The Utah Jazz finished the season with their best record yet, 55 wins and only 27 defeats. Forecasters were picking the team to reach the NBA finals as the Western Conference representative. Team owner Larry Miller announced that financing had been obtained to construct a new $66 million arena for the Jazz in downtown Salt Lake City. The Jazz were flying high as the playoffs started, but were shot down quickly by the underdog Phoenix Suns in the first round, 3 games to 2.

Ground was broken for the new arena, but grumbling from local fans could be heard all across the Rocky Mountains. How could a team boasting Karl Malone as the best power forward and John Stockton as the best point guard play so miserably in the playoffs?

Malone shrugged off the critics, but the playoff failure seemed to linger into the 1990–91 season. Utah struggled, losing seven of its first fifteen games. The team snapped out of it in December and

FACT

Paul Silas, former All-Star NBA forward (1964–80) had this to say about Karl Malone: "He combines brute strength with the ability to run the court. He's like Elvin Hayes, but he's much stronger than Elvin ever was. Karl loves to punish you night after night."

Despite Karl Malone's average of 29 points per game during the series, the Utah Jazz were unable to defeat the Portland Trail Blazers in the 1992 Western Conference Finals.

January. In one nineteen-game stretch in this period, Karl Malone led the team in scoring in every game.

Malone averaged 29 points and 11.8 rebounds during the regular season. Three other Jazz players averaged in double figures—Jeff Malone (18.6), John Stockton (17.2), and Thurl Bailey (12.4). It was a confident group of Utah players that met Phoenix in the first round of the 1991 NBA playoffs. Karl Malone led the Jazz to win the opening game. Utah went on to wrap up the series in four games. Portland was next, and the Trail Blazers proved to be too much. They took care of Utah in five games.

During the 1991–92 season, Malone scored more than forty points in five games during the regular season and carried his team all the way to the Western Conference finals. Unfortunately, Portland defeated the Jazz in six games. Malone averaged 29 points in the playoffs, shooting with an accuracy mark of 52 percent from the field.

In October 1991, Karl Malone was selected to play on the Dream Team. This collection of NBA superstars would represent the United States in the Olympic Games in Barcelona, Spain, in 1992. This would be the first year that American professional basketball players would be allowed to compete in the Olympic Games. At last, Malone had been given the chance to play in the Olympics.

Chapter 6

An Olympic Effort

The most talented group of basketball players ever assembled on one team" was how the sportswriters billed the 1992 United States Olympic team.[1] Not only had Malone been selected, but his greatest ally, John Stockton, also was a member of the Dream Team. "The 1992 U.S. Olympic team exceeded all my hopes and expectations," said Chuck Daly of the Detroit Pistons, the man selected to coach the Dream Team.[2] "They were," Daly recalled, "the highest level of athletes. And one thing they had in common was intelligence. All the people on this team were very, very intelligent about the game."[3]

As for Karl Malone, Daly remarked:

He's an all-star performer who's capable of getting from 25 to 40 points every night. He's as fast a big man as I've ever seen. He has a surprisingly fine shooting touch for a man of his great strength. He's a very physical player, the single strongest person in the league, and a great guy to have on the team.[4]

Karl Malone's talents had been hidden away in the remote state of Utah, but here, at last, he had his chance to perform on the international stage. "The Mailman rarely put on the kind of pyrotechnic displays that most of the other U.S. players did, but Malone always delivered," wrote Cameron Stauth. "That obviously was how he'd earned his famous nickname."[5]

Some would dispute the claim that, at power forward, Karl Malone was the best. On the Dream Team, he joined forces with Charles Barkley, his chief rival for that honor. Both Barkley and Malone refused to make public comparisons of their performances that summer, but Sir Charles did remark, "That Karl Malone is one great player," after the two had dueled head-to-head in one of Daly's private practice sessions.[6]

Finally, it was time to play a real game. The team's first game in Portland was against the Cuban Olympic team. Any doubts about the United States team's ability to compete on the international level were erased in a 136–57 thrashing of Cuba. "After the game," recalled Daly, "I was asked about whether I had tried to slow down our players in order to keep the score from being lopsided. I said that we had to play the game as best as we can, otherwise, why bother?"[7]

Next, the Dream Team blasted Canada, 105–61, and followed that with a 112–52 slaughter of Panama. The fourth game in four nights saw a 128–87 win over Argentina. The South American team played well, but seemed, at times, to be in awe of the Dream Teamers.

On arrival in Spain, the Dream Teamers were treated like rock stars, or, at the very least, royalty. Frenzied crowds stalked them wherever they went, and the Spanish national police force had its hands full trying to keep the fans from ripping the clothes off every player. The crowds were so demanding that, for safety's sake, the team was forced to take residence in a location away from the Olympic Village.

At last it was time for the Olympics to start. Malone, Stockton, and six other players marched in the opening ceremonies. Each was amazed by how exhilarating the experience was. "I wouldn't trade this for anything," Malone said.[8] Then came the first

FACT

The 1992 U.S. Olympic Team members were:

No.	Name
4	Christian Laettner
5	David Robinson
6	Patrick Ewing
7	Larry Bird
8	Scottie Pippen
9	Michael Jordan
10	Clyde Drexler
11	Karl Malone
12	John Stockton
13	Chris Mullin
14	Charles Barkley
15	Magic Johnson

Sharing the spotlight with the rest of the Dream Team in the 1992 Olympics in Barcelona, Spain, Karl Malone represented his country with pride. Most of the Dream Team's opponents were in awe of the NBA stars, and Malone and company had little trouble winning the gold medal.

game. The United States team shot 64 percent and swamped the team from Angola, 116–48. The Americans outscored their opposition 46–1, in one stretch of the first half. Never had the Olympics seen such stellar basketball. Malone, meanwhile, scored a quiet 19 points, making 7 of 10 shots from the field.

Croatia, a formidable opponent, took on the Dream Team next. The star Croatian was Toni Kukoc, who later went on to play for the 1996 Chicago Bulls NBA champion team. The United States team was fired up for the game, more so than for any other before. Croatia, however, had the jitters and persisted in throwing the ball away. Kukoc played one of his worst games. (He hit only 2 of 11 shots.) Jordan's 21 points led the United States in a 103–70 rout. Malone played for only eighteen minutes and had 12 points and 5 rebounds for the Dream Team. The United States would play eight games in the 1992 Olympics, and they had not seen the last of Croatia.

Germany, with future NBA All-Star Detlef Schrempf, was next. Schrempf had been taken higher than Malone in the 1985 draft, going to Dallas, and this was something Karl Malone had never forgotten. Now both were in the international spotlight. Malone outscored Schrempf, 18 to 15. The Dream Team took on Brazil next. By this time, Karl Malone had picked up a powerful friend, heavyweight boxer Evander Holyfield, who sat near the United States bench. Every time, Malone scored or pulled down a rebound, Holyfield would clap and bellow "Karl!" The United States won, 127–83.

The home crowd was spirited for Spain's game with the United States. Spain lost, 122–81. Playing for twenty minutes, Malone grabbed 10 rebounds, four more than Barkley.

Karl Malone was playing better than Sir Charles, but Barkley's bad-boy style and mouth were drawing all the attention. In a way, this mirrored the year-in, year-out competition between the two for best power forward honors.

The Olympic quarterfinals began on August 4, 1992, with the United States flattening Puerto Rico, 115–77. The United States led, 67–40, at halftime, and Malone was needed to play only fifteen minutes. In the semifinals against Lithuania, the United States jumped out to an 11–0 lead despite the intimidating presence of seven-foot three-inch Arvydas Sabonis, who would later star in the NBA for the Portland Trail Blazers. Nine Dream Teamers scored in double figures, including Malone with 18.

The gold medal game pitted the Dream Team against Croatia. The United States team was flat in its warm-up drills. Coach Daly sensed something was wrong, but was unable to rally the troops. This would be a close game, he told assistant P. J. Carlesimo. Before a worldwide television audience, Croatia stunned viewers by actually taking the lead, 25–23, in the first half. Toni Kukoc was a different player than he had been in the first game. Together with teammates Dino Radja and Drazen Petrovic, the Croatians were looking to pull the upset of the century.

Down by two, Coach Daly thought of calling a timeout. He then overruled himself and sat down. There was no need to show his team any signs of panic. Play continued. Barkley pulled up beyond the three-point line and fired. Groans turned to cheers as the ball settled in the basket. The United States never trailed after that, and the team built a 56–42 halftime lead. An exhausted Malone finished the game with 6 points and 4 rebounds. The 1992 Olympics, the greatest sixteen days in Malone's life, were over for the gold medal Dream Team.

Despite playing summer ball at the highest international level, there was no letdown in Karl's performance during the 1992–93 NBA season. He had his second-best year from the field, scoring on 55 percent of his field goal attempts. He was named to the All-NBA First Team for a fifth consecutive season. He scored his sixteen thousandth career point on February 4, 1993, against the Lakers, and also became Utah's all-time leading rebounder. For the season, Karl Malone led the Jazz in rebounding. On February 21, he and Stockton shared Most Valuable Player honors in the NBA All-Star Game played on their home court at the Delta Center. Malone topped the West stars with 28 points and 10 rebounds.

The playoffs came back to haunt the franchise when Utah was eliminated by Seattle in the first round. Malone played his heart out, averaging 24 points and 10 rebounds in the five games, but it was not enough.

As the 1993 training camp opened, the critics blasted the Jazz. According to the critics, the team had peaked several years earlier and was starting a downward drift. Further, Malone and Stockton were simply too worn out from the Olympics and the arduous NBA season to reach their potential in the 1992–93 playoffs.

Karl Malone subsequently led the club to the doorstep of the NBA finals. He and John Stockton showed no signs of slowing down in their ninth season as teammates. But the critics had been right about one thing—Utah was essentially a two-man team. Then, on February 24, 1994, the Jazz traded Jeff Malone and a top draft pick to Philadelphia for

Sean Green and Jeff Hornacek. Green faded into oblivion a month later, but Hornacek went on to become one of the greatest players in Utah history. Hornacek brought a 15-point-per-game average and a hard-nosed, gritty style of play that perfectly complemented Malone and Stockton. Coach Sloan won game number three hundred, and the Jazz finished the regular season with 53 wins and only 29 losses. "He's our Mr. Consistency," Coach Sloan remarked of Karl Malone's performance during the season.

Once again, the playoffs proved to be a disappointment in Salt Lake City. It looked at first like things would be different, when the Jazz came roaring out of the gate to win six of its first seven games. The team disposed of San Antonio, 3 games to one. Then the Jazz took on the Denver Nuggets and won the first three games. Down three games to none in the seven-game Western Conference semifinals, the Nuggets appeared ready to pack it in. All the Jazz had to do was win one more game. But Denver, led by seven-foot two-inch center Dikembe Mutombo, unbelievably forced the series into a seventh game by winning the next three. It took all of Utah's resources to put down the Nuggets, 91–81, in the final game. The Jazz advanced to the conference finals against the Rockets, but clearly Denver had taken the fight out of them. Houston won the series, 4 games to one.

FACT

After Karl Malone won a gold medal in the 1992 Olympics, he gave it to his daughter Kadee. When he won another gold medal in 1996, he gave it to his son, Karl, Jr.

The Utah Jazz became a stronger and more balanced team in 1994, when they acquired Jeff Hornacek in a trade with Philadelphia.

Malone posted another superstar season in 1994–95, finishing fourth in scoring with a 26.7 per game average and ninth in rebounding (10.6 rebounds per game). Malone played in all 82 regular-season NBA contests and took his streak of reaching double figures in points scored to 300 consecutive games.[9] He was selected to his eighth All-Star Game and the All-NBA first team for the seventh time. He finished third in the balloting for Most Valuable Player, behind David Robinson and Shaquille O'Neal.

Karl Malone led Utah to an excellent regular season, winning 60 games for the first time ever. But fate lent a hand in the playoffs, pitting Utah against the eventual NBA champion Houston Rockets in the first round. Houston beat Utah in five games.

Chapter 7

Continued Career Success

As the years passed, Malone grew weary of what he saw to be a change in the way basketball was being played in the NBA. He told friends that he believed the quality of play had eroded since he first arrived in the league.

He said:

I came through at a great time for the game with the guys who wanted to play—the guys who wanted to lay it out there on the line every night. I came by at the perfect time, and I think I'm eventually going to go out at the perfect time.

Now there are a lot of overpaid athletes who don't care about the game. That's the mentality. Back in the old school, guys cared about the game, guys cared about how they treated people. The mentality of players and the way some players approach the game is what's hurting the game. That's what I'm saying. In five years, I think the NBA game is going to suffer.[1]

One of the most successful seasons for the Utah Jazz began at home on November 3, 1995, before a full house of 19,911 fans at the Delta Center. The Jazz coasted to a 112–94 win against the powerful Seattle Supersonics. Malone led the way with 26 points and 11 rebounds. However, in the next game, against the Atlanta Hawks, he dislocated his finger in the first half, but recovered to score 23 points in leading the Jazz to a 105–96 win.

After the game, reporters inquired about Malone's injury, but were assured of his durability by Jazz media relations director Mark Kelly. "In his first ten NBA seasons," Kelly said, "Karl has missed only four games due to injury." Kelly went on to remark that Malone and Stockton combined had missed a total of only eight regular season games.[2]

Malone said:

I take pride in playing. John Stockton takes pride in playing. I see guys get a bruised big toe or a hangnail or a headache, and sometimes they take two or three games off. I don't believe in that.

I think the mentality of some people has hurt the game. If you look around the league right now . . . the attendance is really down. . . .

There are a lot of overpaid athletes [in the NBA] who don't care about the game. You look at some of the older guys—they just went out and played. They took buses, and they went out and played. Now teams are chartering—first-class this and first-class that—and some guys still don't want to play. That's what I'm talking about.[3]

Karl Malone was born to play basketball—to play the game at a level few have reached. The best power forward basketball has ever seen, Malone is out there every game night, running the floor, rebounding, hitting the medium-range jumper, and successfully defending the opposition both inside and out. He is a sure candidate for the Professional Basketball Hall of Fame.

Malone was routinely brilliant in the 1995–96 season, ranking fourth in the league in scoring at 25.8 points per game and eleventh in rebounding at 9.8 rebounds per game. As usual, he started in all 82 games. A typical performance was the one he turned in against the Minnesota Timberwolves. With only fifty-five seconds left in the first quarter, he charged past Minnesota's Christian Laettner, dived for the ball, and crashed into three spectators in the first

Even when he is not in the center of the action on the court, Karl Malone is always aware of what's going on around him, looking for an opportunity to contribute when needed.

row at the Delta Center. Even so, Malone was able to flawlessly slap the ball back into the hands of Stockton, who then hit Utah's first basket for the night. Minnesota offered little resistance after that and fell, 99–83. Malone played only thirty minutes, but he scored 21 points.

Karl Malone was named NBA Player of the Week after he scored 29 points and pulled down 13 rebounds in a 102–92 win over Dallas at Reunion Arena. Then he had 29 points and 11 rebounds, and Utah outscored Portland, 30–8, in the second quarter, to give the Jazz a 96–72 win. Utah's record on January 24 stood at 25 wins and only 13 losses.

Malone hit for 39 points at the Forum in Inglewood, California, against the Lakers, but Los Angeles had a new weapon, a "super sub" named Earvin "Magic" Johnson, who returned from retirement to spark his team to a 110–103 win. Magic came off the bench for his strongest performance (21 points) in the third game of his 1996 comeback.

Malone could only marvel at Magic's performance. Johnson was one of the players from the old school that Malone admired. Although Magic rejoined the Lakers as a player, a few seasons earlier the new wave of NBA players had so soured him on coaching, that he left after only a month on the job. "The young guys," Magic said, "cared more about their cell phones and beepers than about how to play the game."[4]

Meanwhile Karl Malone just kept rolling along. He registered the first triple double of his career against the Los Angeles Clippers at the Delta Center. (A triple double occurs when a player scores in double figures in any three of the following: points, rebounds, assists, and steals.) Against the Clippers, Malone had 27 points, 15 rebounds, and 10 assists.

Next it was John Stockton's turn to make history by breaking Maurice Cheeks's record for career steals in a game against the Boston Celtics at the Delta Center. Stockton, who set the NBA career record for assists a year earlier, entered the game with 2,309 steals, one shy of the record Cheeks built in fifteen seasons. Next, Malone had 26 points and 14 rebounds as Utah waltzed past Toronto, 102–96.

A reporter asked Karl Malone about his greatest thrill in basketball. Without hesitation, he replied, "Taking the pass from John Stockton and making the shot for his all-time assist record."[5]

By this time, Malone and Stockton were as linked as two peas in a pod. The duo had become inseparable in the public's mind. But, would Malone be just as good a player without the services of Stockton? Most observers think that one could not perform without the other. "Nonsense," said

Minnesota Timberwolves coach Phil "Flip" Saunders. "Malone doesn't need Stockton. Karl would be a fabulous player with anyone playing point guard. Stockton is a good complement to Malone, but Karl would be an All-Star on any team."[6]

Fans of the Utah Jazz approached the 1996 play-offs with trepidation. Fresh in their memories was the previous year's first-round loss to the Houston Rockets. What would this year bring?

Karl Malone had this to say to NBA writer Fran Blinebury of the *Houston Chronicle*:

> It's all about doing whatever I can do to win a championship. That's what's driving me now. The Jazz have given me the opportunity to make a good living for my family and for my future. But whether I am a truck driver, a rancher, or an athlete, I will still be giving my all, busting my butt every day. I don't coast. It is a disgrace to God not to use the full potential you have been given.[7]

The Portland Trail Blazers arrived in Salt Lake City for Game 1 and immediately met the determined duo of Malone and Stockton. Neither of the men was getting any younger, and both indicated this would be Utah's year to win the championship. In the game at the Delta Center, Stockton had 23 assists, one short of his previous playoff record, and

While some have questioned whether Karl Malone would be the same player without outstanding teammates such as John Stockton, others like Minnesota Timberwolves coach Phil Saunders (pictured here) think that Malone would be a star no matter where he played.

Malone scored 33 points and recorded 9 rebounds, to set the table for the rest of the series. The Jazz won, 110–102.

Utah kept up the heat in the second game. After the first half ended in a 50–50 tie, Malone and Stockton rallied the Jazz to a 105–90 victory. Malone had 30 points and 14 rebounds. Stockton registered 16 assists and 15 points. The series moved to Portland for Game 3. The Trail Blazers were not about to go down without a fight. Portland won, 94–91, despite Malone's 35 points.

Portland tied the series at two games apiece with another win at the Rose Garden. Malone had a terrible night, hitting only 4 of 16 from the field and 7 for 12 from the free-throw line. The series would return to Salt Lake City for the fifth and deciding game. There would be no first-round elimination for the Jazz in the 1996 playoffs. Utah crushed the Trail Blazers, 102–64. The Jazz held Portland to the lowest point total in the forty-nine-year history of the NBA playoffs.

This set the stage for the conference semifinals against Midwest Division champion San Antonio. Because the Spurs had won their division, they were awarded home court advantage. This meant the first two games would be played in Texas's Alamodome. Veteran NBA observers gave the Jazz little chance in the first game, but Malone and Stockton paced Utah to a lopsided 95–75 win over the stunned Spurs. Malone scored 23 points, and Stockton had 13 points and 19 assists. But it was Utah's suffocating defense that won the game. "Our defense stepped up again," Jeff Hornacek said. "We made them take tough shots."[8]

The Spurs' seven-foot one-inch, 250-pound center, David Robinson, responded to the Jazz's challenge by scoring 24 points and pulling down 12 rebounds as San Antonio won the second game, 88–77. The series moved to Delta Center, where Utah won easily, 105–75. Malone, who sat out the fourth quarter, was 14 for 24 from the field and grabbed 11 rebounds.

Another blowout victory was recorded by Utah in the fourth game. The team was playing the best ball of any team in Jazz franchise history. The team's three victories over the Spurs were by twenty, thirty, and fifteen points, highly unusual in the tightly contested NBA playoffs. Privately, Utah fans were daring to hope that this could be a championship year. After San Antonio brought the Jazz and their fans back to earth with a victory, the series went back to Salt Lake for Game 6.

Malone and Stockton agreed that the series would come to an end in the Delta Center, and they made good on their promise. The Jazz made it back to the conference finals for the third time in five years, with a 108–81 smashing of the Spurs. Malone had 25 points and 12 rebounds. "I said our bench would make the difference at some point," Malone told reporters after the game, "and these guys really stepped it up."[9]

NBA officials, ever mindful of television's impact, scheduled the first game of the conference finals less than thirty-six hours after the Jazz eliminated the Spurs. Television was also on Malone's mind when he announced before the game that he would not speak to NBC reporters. He considered it retribution for the network's previous neglect of the Jazz. Not once had NBC scheduled a regular-season Utah game for nationwide broadcast. To Malone, it seemed that NBC believed the Utah Jazz did not exist. This was his way of telling the network what he thought of its scheduling policies. But Jazz president Frank Layden could see NBC's point. "From a practical standpoint," Layden said, "we're just a smaller market."[10] "Out of sight, out of mind" appeared to be the network philosophy.

Utah was facing the Seattle Supersonics, a team that had outplayed them all season. Seattle had won 64 games in the regular season, second best in the NBA after the Chicago Bulls. The Sonics had easily eliminated two-time defending champion Houston with a four-game sweep. In the first game of the divisional championship series, a tired Utah team fell behind, 24–23, at the end of the first quarter, and then fell apart. Seattle romped to a 102–72 win. The thirty-point loss was the worst defeat of the season for the Jazz, and no other Utah team had ever lost a playoff game by thirty points. Team members could only hang their heads in shame. "It looked like Seattle had 10 guys guarding us out there today," commented Coach Sloan. "They beat us every way you can in a game."[11]

While Utah played better in the next game, Seattle still won, 91–87. The Jazz could not wait to get back to the friendly confines of the Delta Center for Game 3. Their backs were against the wall, and each team member knew it. Cable network TNT broadcast the game, so those who did not have access to cable television were denied the opportunity to view the action. What they missed was a furious Karl Malone playing at the height of his ability. That night, Malone would record 28 points and 18 rebounds. "In the first quarter," Malone recalled in the locker room afterward, "everyone was uptight. I tried to get something going and let everyone feed off me. Then we settled down and let the game come to us."[12]

NBC announced that it would indeed televise Game 4 at the Delta Center. Malone had finally caught the attention of the previously uninterested network bosses. "It turned into a pride thing," Malone observed.[13] He knew Utah had to keep on winning to stay before NBC cameras.

It will forever be known in Salt Lake City as the shot that missed. Utah trailed Seattle, 88–86, with two seconds left in the game. John Stockton was the shooter from three-point range. The ball left his hand and flew in a perfect arc toward the basket. Not a soul in the Delta Center thought it would miss. It appeared it would hit nothing but net. But then the perfect shot went astray, hit the rim, and bounced away. The Jazz had lost and trailed Seattle, 3 games to one. Moreover, the series was moving to Seattle, where the Sonics had been invincible in 1996.

Then, in their finest hour in franchise history, the Utah Jazz came back from the dead. They won a road game in the conference finals for the first time ever, 98–95, in overtime at Key Arena.

Malone said:

> We said that this team always responds when things are tough on us. We always believed in ourselves when everyone else didn't. It's amazing what you can do when you put your mind to it.[14]

In order to reach the 1996 NBA finals, the Utah Jazz would have to overcome a strong Seattle SuperSonics team in the Western Conference Finals.

Game 6 was to see the Jazz slaughter Seattle, 108–83. Playing like men possessed by demons, the Jazz roared past the Supersonics as if they were standing still. Malone had 32 points, 10 rebounds, and 7 assists. The crowd at the Delta Center spent most of the game on their feet, screaming approval. Never had a Utah team done so well in a crucial game. At the end, the crowd cheered itself hoarse with multiple standing ovations.

The seventh and deciding game, of course, would be played at Key Arena in Seattle. This was the result of the Sonics' superior 64–18 regular-season record. This is how the NBA determines home court advantage. Malone and Stockton did all they could to see that Utah stayed alive in the 1996 championship race. Unfortunately, it was not enough. In the end, the Sonics managed to hold off a desperate last-ditch final flurry mounted by the Jazz after the team trailed, 85–77. Stockton's shot from the lane capped a 7–0 Jazz run, to make it 85–84. Then, twice fouled as he moved toward the basket, Seattle power forward Shawn Kemp sank four free throws to ice the game. In victory, a gracious Kemp had kind words for his adversary, Malone. "What's amazing," Kemp said, "is that every time he gets the ball down low, he scores a field goal, or gets to the line. He's automatic."[15]

Chapter 8

Can the Mailman Deliver?

Even though the chase for the NBA title had ended, Karl Malone would find himself playing basketball until August. There was no question; he would be invited back for the 1996 Olympics as a member of the second Olympic Dream Team.

Others from the 1992 team had retired or fallen by the wayside, but Malone and John Stockton were immediately invited to return. (Charles Barkley was a last-minute addition to the team.) Other returning Dream Teamers were Scottie Pippen and David Robinson. New to the team were Hakeem Olajuwon, Shaquille O'Neal, Mitch Richmond, Gary Payton, Reggie Miller, Grant Hill, and Anfernee "Penny" Hardaway.

This was to be a different experience than the first time around. For one thing, the Olympics were staged in the United States, in Atlanta, Georgia. The international atmosphere present in a foreign country was missing. For the Dream Team, it was as if every game were a home game. Indeed, the coach of the 1996 U.S. Olympic team was Lenny Wilkens, coach of the hometown Atlanta Hawks.

A funny thing happened to the Dream Team in the 1996 Olympics—they were judged to be too good. The experience of the 1992 team led fans to believe that the 1996 group would swamp the opposition. This led to a concern expressed by some that, in the future, perhaps United States basketball players should be amateurs. This is absolutely outlandish in view of the fact that these were the same people clamoring for professional representation after Russia and Yugoslavia had won gold medals in the past. The adulation of Barcelona was missing in Atlanta; the Dream Team had, in fact, become old hat. Nevertheless, team members went about their business and captured a second gold medal for the United States of America.

Until the gold medal game against Yugoslavia, the Dream Team met no serious opposition, but the early games lacked excitement. Said Jan Hubbard, executive editor of *Hoop* magazine:

In 1996, the international teams were more patient, content to use as much of the 30-second clock as possible. They also were dedicated to getting back on defense. The result was the 1996 Dream Team was unable to run as much as the 1992 team, and that made the games closer.[1]

Against Argentina, the Dream Team allowed the opposition to score from the outside and, as a result, led by only two points, 46–44, at halftime. It was clear that the days of total domination over other countries was at an end. Then, as if by magic, the lethargic United States team awoke to outscore the Argentineans and come away 96–68 victors.

Malone took it upon himself to pull the Dream Team out of its funk by scoring 12 points, to lead the United States to a convincing 87–54 win over Angola. The Angolans stalled out their possessions in an attempt to hold the United States under 100 points. With no player taller than six feet six inches, Angola shot mostly from the perimeter.

Karl Malone scored 14 points in the next victory, 104–82, over Lithuania. Charles Barkley came alive to lead all scorers with 16 points. "It's not going to be like 1992," Malone said after the contest. "We have lost the 'awe factor' we had going then. Teams in 1992 were just in awe of us."[2] Late in the game, Malone cut a finger on the rim attempting to block a

The second Olympic Dream Team repeated as gold medal-winners in the 1996 Olympic Games in Atlanta. Though this Dream Team was not as close to the center of attention as the first one, players such as Karl Malone still managed to put on an impressive show for the fans.

shot, and five stitches were needed to close the wound. He was "questionable" for the next game, according to Coach Wilkens. But, showing absolutely no signs of wear or injury, Malone, with teammate Scottie Pippen, scored the first fourteen points for the Dream Team in their next game, as the United States trounced China, 133–70, for its fourth win. The hand injury was no problem, Karl Malone told reporters.

Next was Croatia and Toni Kukoc, now a member of the NBA champion Chicago Bulls. Pippen showed Kukoc who was the better Bull as he outplayed his Croatian teammate, and the United States won the game, 102–71, to advance to the Olympic quarterfinals. Malone contributed 10 points to the win.

The quarterfinal opponent was Brazil, with Oscar Schmidt, the most prolific scorer in international basketball history. Schmidt shot 8 for 20 from the field and scored 26 points, but his supporting cast was not near Dream Team caliber, and Brazil lost, 98–75. Their only consolation was that Brazil held the United States team under 100 points. Malone played sparingly and had only 9 points for the Dream Team.

Utah coach and Dream Team assistant Jerry Sloan said:

These teams have a different style of play. They have learned that they can keep the game closer by running as much time off the clock as possible. They also don't have a lot of big inside players like Karl Malone, so that forces them to learn to play the game on the perimeter.[3]

The semifinals pitted the United States against Australia, the hottest shooting team in the tournament. A crowd of 34,068 at the Georgia Dome saw the United States fall behind by four points, with seven minutes left in the first half. Australia, led by three-point specialist Shane Heal, scored on its fifth consecutive possession. This seemed to anger the Dream Team, as it went on a 13–2 run to lead by 51–41 at halftime. The second half was no contest as the United States buried Australia and won, 101–73.

"The gap is getting closer," Coach Wilkens responded when asked if he thought the other countries could someday defeat a United States Dream Team of professionals in Olympic competition.[4] Some thought it could happen in the 1996 gold medal game. "Instead of 40-point wins," Malone said, "we may be winning by only 25. But you have to remember that, number one, we haven't played very well, and, number two, we are still winning."[5]

The gold medal game was to be played against Yugoslavia, whose best player was Charlotte Hornet center Vlade Divac. The Americans could not hold any kind of lead during the first sixteen minutes of the game, and it looked like the Yugoslavian team was capable of pulling off an upset. Divac was playing like a man on a mission. He elbowed Malone out of the way on several rebound attempts. Then, in the final six minutes of the first half, the Dream Team's offense came alive and outscored Yugoslavia, 14–4. At halftime, the scoreboard read: United States 43, Yugoslavia 38. The Dream Team then started off the second half with a barrage of scoring, and the Yugoslavian team uncharacteristically threw the ball away several times. The United States outscored them, 52–31, in the period, for a 95–69 victory and the gold medal.

For Malone, his second gold medal was his proudest accomplishment. He compared the two Olympic teams:

> From now on, I guess every team will be compared to that 1992 team. Still, I think the 1996 team made its own identity on defense. In 1992, we knew we were going to blow teams out. But in 1996, we were more interested in shutting teams down. That's why we dominated in the second half of all our games this year.[6]

For Malone, the 1996–97 NBA season began with an important announcement from league headquarters. As part of the NBA's fiftieth anniversary, Karl Malone was named as one of the fifty greatest players in league history. Thus, the name of Karl Malone was joined with such lasting legends of the game as Michael Jordan, Wilt Chamberlain, Bill Russell, Kareem Abdul-Jabbar, Larry Bird, George Mikan, and Magic Johnson.

Malone was surprised by his selection. He believed he might be ignored because he had spent his entire pro career in the remote, small market of Salt Lake City, and his team had yet to win an NBA championship. The tremendous honor of being selected and the near-miss in the 1996 playoffs both served to add incentive to Malone's quest for an NBA championship ring.

Something else was driving him, too—something involving a white porcelain angel that now sits in Malone's locker at the Delta Center. During the previous season, Malone had been introduced to Danny Ewing, a young boy suffering from terminal leukemia. Throughout his professional career, and with little publicity, Karl Malone had always taken the time to visit the children's wards of hospitals in cities he visited. One such visit brought him into contact with young Ewing, who touched Malone deeply. He wanted the boy to fly to the Olympics with him, but Danny was simply too ill. He did not have long to live. Before he died, Danny gave Karl Malone the porcelain angel that he now keeps in his locker. "I'll be your angel now, Karl Malone," Danny had told him. "I'll be watching over you."[7]

After the Olympics, most of the Dream Team headed for the beach, but not Malone. In a toolshed on his Arkansas ranch, he embarked on a self-imposed weight lifting program. Even though the temperature often exceeded 100 degrees, Karl Malone stuck to his regimen. "I hate air-conditioned gyms," he told his wife, Kay.[8] When he was not lifting weights, he was running up and down the stadium steps at the local high school football field.

"I can't wait," Malone told his wife. "I know exactly where the [NBA] Most Valuable Player trophy is going—on the mantle right over the stone fireplace. Every time I walk by it, I'll touch it."[9] The Most Valuable Player trophy, Malone reasoned, had been twelve years in coming. In 1996–97, he had the season of his life. And he owed it all to a guardian angel in the shape of a white porcelain figurine.

Still, individual attention continued to elude him. At age thirty-three, in his twelfth season with the Jazz, with a lifetime average of 26 points and 10 rebounds per game, he felt he deserved more nationwide respect. He saw a glaring example of this when fans voting for the Western Conference

All-Star team bypassed him in favor of Shawn Kemp of the SuperSonics.

Karl Malone admitted he was disappointed when Kemp outpaced him by more than 375,000 votes, but remarked that he no longer needed fan appreciation. "It has to do with television commercials," he told Jackie MacMullan of *Sports Illustrated.* "If people see your face a lot, and you put up decent numbers, you're set. I don't get invited to play in charity games, and I don't play golf. I don't go to Las Vegas or Atlantic City."[10]

In Boston, on March 19, 1997, Malone played just the first three quarters against the Celtics. He scored 32 points and moved into tenth place on the NBA's all-time scoring list in Utah's 113–100 victory. With 25,414 points, he passed Laker legend Jerry West (25,192) to move into the top ten. Earlier in the month, Karl Malone became just the fifth player to reach 25,000 points and 10,000 rebounds, joining Wilt Chamberlain, Kareem Abdul-Jabbar, Moses Malone, and Elvin Hayes. Abdul-Jabbar tops the scoring list with 38,387 points, followed by Chamberlain (31,419), Moses Malone (27,409), and Hayes (27,409). Next come Michael Jordan, Oscar Robertson, Dominique Wilkins, John Havlicek, Alex English, and Karl Malone.

In a 118–114 Utah victory over the Toronto Raptors,

FACT

Karl Malone and his wife, Kay, are the parents of two daughters and a son. They make their home in Salt Lake City. Kay Malone is a former Miss Idaho, USA.

After many years of playing basketball, Karl Malone continues to play each game with the same intensity that he did when he was a rookie. As long as he continues to do so, he will likely remain a favorite among the fans in Salt Lake City and beyond.

Karl Malone turned in his second triple-double with 32 points, 13 rebounds, and 10 assists. Next, he hit for 41 points in a 111–104 road win over the Golden State Warriors. Four nights later, he scored 41 points yet again in a 95–88 home win over the Pistons. "Karl Malone," Pistons coach Doug Collins said, "is as consistent as running water."[11]

Karl Malone won his first-ever NBA Most Valuable Player award in May of 1997. Malone unseated Chicago Bulls superstar Michael Jordan for the league's top honor.

Of the 107 respondents who revealed their selection to the *Deseret News*, 65 said Malone was their top choice. Jordan, who received 42 votes, was the first player in seventeen years of media voting to get more than 40 votes but not win, the newspaper reported.

Malone led the Jazz to a franchise-best 64 wins and top seed in the Western Conference. He averaged 27.4 points per game and 9.9 rebounds per game during the 1996–97 NBA season. The Jazz lost the 1997 Finals to the Chicago Bulls in six games. Malone averaged 23.8 points per game during the Finals.

He had two more seasons left on his contract with the Utah Jazz and a reported unwritten agreement with team owner Larry Miller to play an additional year for the team.

"Malone admits," wrote MacMullan in *Sports Illustrated*, "that he daydreams about playing for other teams on which the load would be lighter and the rewards might be greater." MacMullan asked Malone about the future. Smiling, Malone replied, "We'll see."[12]

There was also the possibility that Malone might retire from the game completely after his contractual obligations were honored. "I have a small real estate company now," he said, "and a Toyota dealership. I plan to open up a Honda dealership, too. I just want to hunt and fish and watch my kids grow up. When the game is over, the game is over."[13]

Chapter Notes

Chapter 1

1. Jerry Zgoda, "Malone, Stockton Steal the Show," *Minneapolis Star Tribune*, February 22, 1993, p. 1C.

2. Ibid.

Chapter 2

1. Cameron Stauth, *The Golden Boys* (New York: Simon & Schuster, Inc., 1992), p. 238.

2. Howard Blatt, *Dream Team II* (New York: Simon & Schuster, Inc., 1996), p. 96.

3. Ibid.

4. Steve Luhm, "Jazz's Mailman Delivers in a Big Way," *Hoop,* March 1988, p. 2.

5. Ibid.

6. Ibid.

7. Luhm, p. 2.

8. Stauth, p. 239.

9. Ibid.

10. Ibid.

11. Blatt, p. 98.

12. Stauth, p. 239.

13. Ibid.

Chapter 3

1. Howard Blatt, *Dream Team II* (New York: Simon & Schuster, Inc., 1996), p. 98.

2. Ibid.

3. Keith Prince, *Dogs Try for Bigger Bite* (Ruston, La.: Louisiana Tech University Press, 1984), p. 4.

4. Ibid.

5. *Sports Heroes, Feats and Facts* (Stamford, Conn.: Master Publishers, 1996), p. 3.

6. Prince, p. 5.

7. Ibid.

8. Ibid.

Chapter 4

1. Steve Luhm, "Jazz's Mailman Delivers in a Big Way," *Hoop*, March 1988, p. 2.

2. Ibid., p. 4.

3. Ibid.

4. Ibid.

5. Cameron Stauth, *The Golden Boys* (New York: Simon & Schuster, Inc., 1992), p. 240.

6. Luhm, p. 6.

7. Stauth, p. 240.

8. Kraig Kragthorpe, "Karl Malone Utah's Jazzy Young Leader," *Basketball Digest*, January 1988, p. 19.

9. Luhm, p. 4.

Chapter 5

1. Cameron Stauth, *The Golden Boys* (New York: Simon & Schuster, Inc., 1992), p. 241.

2. Kraig Kragthorpe, "Karl Malone Utah's Jazzy Young Leader," *Basketball Digest*, January 1988, p. 22.

3. William Ladson, "You Have to Be Nasty to Survive in the NBA," *Sport*, May, 1992, p. 50.

Chapter 6

1. "Dream Team Gets Ready to Take on the World," Post Cereals Publications, Summer 1992, unpaged.

2. Chuck Daly and Alex Sachare, *America's Dream Team: The Quest for Olympic Gold* (New York: High-Top Publications Book on Audio Tape, 1993).

3. Ibid.

4. Ibid.

5. Cameron Stauth, *The Golden Boys* (New York: Simon & Schuster, Inc., 1992), p. 364.

6. Charles Barkley and Roy S. Johnson, *Outrageous* (New York: Avon Books, 1992), p. 338.

7. Daly and Sachare.

8. Ibid.

9. Minnesota Timberwolves NBA Game Notes, Minnesota Timberwolves Media Relations Department, April 18, 1995.

Chapter 7

1. Barry M. Bloom, "NBA Star Karl Malone Speaks Out," ESPN Inc. and Starwave Corporation, 1996, p. 1.

2. Mark Kelly, *I Love Basketball* (Salt Lake City, Utah: Utah Jazz Public Relations Department, 1996), p. 53.

3. Bloom, p. 2.

4. Ibid.

5. "One on One With Karl Malone," ESPN, Inc., and Starwave Corporation, February 8, 1997, p. 14.

6. Author interview with Phil Saunders, October 3, 1996.

7. Fran Blinebury, "Profiles of 10 of Pro Basketball's Top Players," *Street & Smith's Pro Basketball*, 1996, p. 36.

8. Associated Press, "Utah 95, San Antonio 75," *Minneapolis Star Tribune*, May 8, 1996, p. C3.

9. "Jazz Ends Spurs' Season," *Minneapolis Star Tribune*, May 17, 1996, p. C6.

10. "Small-Market Woes Have Jazz Singing Blues," *Athlon Sports Pro Basketball Edition*, 1996, p. 121.

11. "Sonics are Super in Opening Romp," *Minneapolis Star Tribune*, May 19, 1996, p. C8.

12. Associated Press, "Utah 96, Seattle 76," *Minneapolis Star Tribune*, May 25, 1996, p. C4.

13. Ibid.

14. "Clincher Eludes Sonics in OT," *Minneapolis Star Tribune*, May 29, 1996, p. C7.

15. ESPN-TV Sports Center interview with Shawn Kemp, June 2, 1996.

Chapter 8

1. Jan Hubbard, "Still Golden," *Hoop*, Fall 1996, p. 5.

2. Dan Barreiro, "Dream Team Overcomes Slow Start," *Minneapolis Star Tribune*, July 25, 1996, p. S4.

3. Hubbard, p. 8.

4. Ibid.

5. Associated Press, "U.S. 101, Australia 73," *Minneapolis Star Tribune*, p. S6.

6. Hubbard, p. 9.

7. Tom Friend, "Keeping Watch Over an M.V.P. Dream," *The New York Times*, April 22, 1997, p. B13.

8. Ibid., p. B16.

9. Ibid.

10. Jackie MacMullan, "The Jazz Master," *Sports Illustrated*, March 17, 1997, p. 101.

11. Ibid., p. 102.

12. Ibid.

13. "One on One with Karl Malone," ESPN, Inc., and Starwave Corporation, February 8, 1997, p. 14.

Career Statistics

YEAR	TEAM	G	FG%	REB	AST	STL	BLK	PTS	AVG
1985–86	Jazz	81	.496	718	236	105	44	1,203	14.9
1986–87	Jazz	82	.512	855	158	104	60	1,779	21.7
1987–88	Jazz	82	.520	986	199	117	50	2,268	27.7
1988–89	Jazz	80	.519	853	219	144	70	2,326	29.1
1989–90	Jazz	82	.562	911	226	121	50	2,540	31.0
1990–91	Jazz	82	.527	967	270	89	79	2,382	29.0
1991–92	Jazz	81	.526	909	241	108	51	2,272	28.0
1992–93	Jazz	82	.552	919	308	124	85	2,217	27.0
1993–94	Jazz	82	.497	940	328	125	126	2,063	25.2
1994–95	Jazz	82	.536	871	285	129	85	2,187	26.7
1995–96	Jazz	82	.519	804	345	138	56	2,106	25.7
1996–97	Jazz	82	.550	803	367	113	48	2,249	27.4
Totals		980	.527	10,536	3,182	1,417	804	25,592	26.1

G—Games Played
FG%—Field Goals Percentage
REB—Rebound
AST—Assists

STL—Steals
BLK—Blocks
PTS—Points
AVG—Point Average

Where to Write
Karl Malone

Mr. Karl Malone
c/o Utah Jazz
The Delta Center
301 West South Temple
Salt Lake City, UT 84101

Index

DISCARDED
PROPERTY OF
KINSMAN FREE PUBLIC LIBRARY